TO: Aunt Clara

FROM: ~~Betsy~~

DATE: 12-19-2015

"I Know the **PLANS I HAVE FOR YOU,**" *Says the Lord*

HARVEST HOUSE PUBLISHERS
EUGENE, OREGON

"I Know the Plans I Have for You," Says the Lord

Text copyright © 2015 by Harvest House Publishers

Published by Harvest House Publishers
Eugene, Oregon 97402
www.harvesthousepublishers.com

ISBN 978-0-7369-6406-7

Design and production by Dugan Design Group,
Bloomington, Minnesota

Harvest House Publishers has made every effort to trace the ownership of all poems and quotes. In the event of a question arising from the use of a poem or quote, we regret any error made and will be pleased to make the necessary correction in future editions of this book.

All Scripture verses are taken from *The Living Bible*, Copyright © 1971. Used by permission of Tyndale House Publishers, Inc., Wheaton, IL 60189 USA. All rights reserved.

Printed in China.

14 15 16 17 18 19 20 21 22 23 /DS/ 10 9 8 7 6 5 4 3 2 1

"I Know the **PLANS** I HAVE FOR YOU," Says the Lord.

"THEY ARE PLANS FOR GOOD AND NOT FOR EVIL, TO GIVE YOU A FUTURE AND A HOPE."

JEREMIAH 29:11

BEHIND *the* DIM UNKNOWN, STANDETH GOD WITHIN THE SHADOW, KEEPING WATCH ABOVE HIS *Own.*

JAMES RUSSELL LOWELL

To accomplish great things, we must
not only act, but also dream; not only plan,
but also believe.

ANATOLE FRANCE

As well could you expect a plant to grow
without air and water as to expect your heart
to grow without prayer and faith.

CHARLES H. SPURGEON

The foolish fears of what might happen,
    I cast them all away
Among the clover-scented grass,
    Among the new mown hay,
Among the husking of the corn,
    Where drowsy poppies nod,
Where ill thoughts die and good are born—
    Out in the fields with God.

ELIZABETH BARRETT BROWNING AND
LOUISE IMOGEN GUINEY

Lord, when doubts fill my mind, when
my heart is in turmoil, quiet me and give me
renewed hope and cheer.

PSALM 94:19

Peace like the river's gentle flow,
Peace like the morning's silent glow,
From day to day, in love supplied,
An endless and unebbing tide.

HORATIUS BONAR

A happy life consists in tranquility of mind.

CICERO

Life is good!

SPRING

IN THE

WORLD!

AND ALL THINGS ARE

Made New!

RICHARD HOVEY

HE WILL HELP YOU

in all your trials; you will find

HIM

EVERYWHERE.

Encouragement costs you nothing to give, but it is priceless to receive.

AUTHOR UNKNOWN

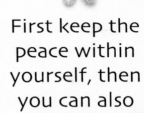

First keep the peace within yourself, then you can also bring peace to others.

THOMAS À KEMPIS

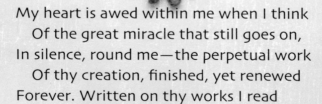

My heart is awed within me when I think
Of the great miracle that still goes on,
In silence, round me—the perpetual work
Of thy creation, finished, yet renewed
Forever. Written on thy works I read
The lesson of thy own eternity.

WILLIAM CULLEN BRYANT

I'm not afraid of storms,
for I'm learning how to sail my ship.

LOUISA MAY ALCOTT

When I am afraid, I will put my confidence in
you. Yes, I will trust the promises of God.

PSALM 56:3

The very word "God" suggests
care, kindness, goodness; and the idea
of God in his infinity is infinite
care, infinite kindness, infinite
goodness. We give God the name of good; it is
only by shortening it that it becomes God.

HENRY WARD BEECHER

Do not seek to understand in order that
you may believe, but believe so that you
may understand.

AUGUSTINE OF HIPPO

Nothing
IS WORTH MORE
than
This Day.

Johann Wolfgang von Goethe

Find Joy
IN THE
Moment!

In the end, it's not the years in
your life that count.
It's the life in your years.

ABRAHAM LINCOLN

All love is sweet, given or returned.
Common as light is love,
And its familiar voice wearies not ever.
They who inspire it most are fortunate,
As I am now: but those who feel it most
Are happier still.

PERCY BYSSHE SHELLEY

Do not wait for extraordinary
circumstances to do good;
try to use ordinary situations.

JEAN PAUL RICHTER

Every action of our lives touches
on some chord that will vibrate
in eternity.

EDWIN HUBBELL CHAPIN

All I have seen teaches me to trust
the creator for all I have not seen.

RALPH WALDO EMERSON

He sendeth sun, he sendeth shower,
Alike they're needful for the flower;
And joys and tears alike are sent
To give the soul fit nourishment.

SARAH FLOWER ADAMS

Now God be praised, that to
believing souls
Gives light in darkness,
comfort in despair!

WILLIAM SHAKESPEARE

THE SOUL IS STRONG THAT TRUSTS IN *Goodness.*

Philip Massinger

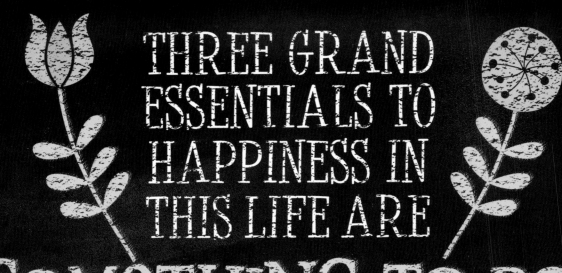

THREE GRAND ESSENTIALS TO HAPPINESS IN THIS LIFE ARE

SOMETHING TO DO,

SOMETHING TO LOVE

and something to hope for

JOSEPH ADDISON

We are shaped and
fashioned
by what we love.

JOHANN WOLFGANG VON GOETHE

Dost thou love life?
Then do not
squander time, for that
is the stuff
life is made of.

BENJAMIN FRANKLIN

No worries!

Live for something. Do good, and leave behind you a monument of virtue that the storms of time can never destroy. Write your name in kindness, love, and mercy on the hearts of thousands you come in contact with year by year, and you will never be forgotten. Your name and your good deeds will shine as the stars of heaven.

THOMAS CHALMERS

When you enjoy becoming wise, there is hope for you! A bright future lies ahead!

PROVERBS 24:13

Hope is the thing with feathers, that perches in the soul, and sings the tune without words, and never stops at all.

EMILY DICKINSON

THE ART OF

Being Happy

LIES IN
THE POWER OF
EXTRACTING
HAPPINESS

from

COMMON THINGS.

HENRY WARD BEECHER

The older I get, the greater power I seem
to have to help the world; I am like a
snowball—the further I am rolled,
the more I gain.

SUSAN B. ANTHONY

Lovely flowers are the smiles
of God's goodness.

WILLIAM WILBERFORCE

The level of our success is limited
only by our imagination
and no act of
kindness, however
small, is ever
wasted.

AESOP

I try to avoid
looking
backward
and keep
looking upward.

CHARLOTTE
BRONTË

20

EVERY MAN'S
LIFE
IS A
Fairy-Tale
WRITTEN BY
GOD'S
FINGERS.

← HANS CHRISTIAN ANDERSEN →

Faith Goes Up the Stairs That Love Has Made & LOOKS OUT THE WINDOW WHICH HOPE HAS OPENED.

CHARLES H. SPURGEON

Don't worry when
you are not recognized, but strive to be
worthy of recognition.

A BRAHAM   L INCOLN

As every thread of gold is valuable, so is every
moment of time.

J OHN   M ASON

Trust the past to God's mercy, the present to God's love
and the future to God's providence.

A UGUSTINE   OF   H IPPO

It will all work out okay.

Happiness
is a choice
THAT REQUIRES
effort
AT TIMES. *Aeschylus*

Without courage,
wisdom bears no fruit.

AUTHOR UNKNOWN

Faith, mighty faith, the promise sees
And looks to that alone;
Laughs at impossibilities,
And cries, "It shall be done!"

CHARLES WESLEY

No dreamer is ever too small;
no dream
is ever too big.

AUTHOR UNKNOWN

Happiness resides not in possessions
and not in gold; the feeling of happiness
dwells in the soul.

DEMOCRITUS

His Way is
PEACEFUL.

Then I lay down and
slept in peace and woke
up safely, for the Lord was
watching over me.

PSALM 3:5

O God of peace,
thy peace impart
To every troubled
trembling heart.

HORATIUS BONAR

There are souls in this world who have the
gift of finding joy everywhere, and leaving
it behind them when they go.

FREDERICK WILLIAM FABER

HE Fills Me WITH STRENGTH and PROTECTS ME

WHEREVER I GO.

Psalm 18:32

One must not always think
so much about what one
should do, but rather what
one should be.
Our works do not ennoble
us; but we must ennoble
our works.

ECKHART VON HOCHHEIM

I feel an earnest and
humble desire, and shall
till I die, to increase
the stock of harmless
cheerfulness.

CHARLES DICKENS

He started to sing as he tackled the thing
That couldn't be done, and he did it.

EDGAR A. GUEST

Nothing great was ever done
without much enduring.

CATHERINE OF SIENA

He is a wise man who does not
grieve for the things which he has not,
but rejoices for those which he has.

EPICTETUS

To look up and not down,
To look forward and not back,
To look out and not in, and
To lend a hand.

EDWARD EVERETT HALE

ALL GOD'S PLEASURES
ARE SIMPLE ONES; HEALTH,
THE RAPTURE OF A MAY MORNING,
SUNSHINE,
THE STREAM BLUE AND GREEN,
kind words,
BENEVOLENT ACTS, THE GLOW OF GOOD HUMOR.

F.W. ROBERTSON

We know how much God loves
us because we have felt his love
and because we believe him when he
tells us that he loves us dearly.

1 JOHN 4:16

Smooth seas do not
make skillful sailors.

AFRICAN PROVERB

Life is made up, not of great sacrifices
or duties, but of little things, in
which smiles and kindness, and small
obligations given habitually, are what
win and preserve the heart, and
secure comfort.

SIR H. DAVY

In actual life every great enterprise begins with and takes its first forward step in faith.

AUGUST WILHELM VON SCHLEGEL

We have not received the Spirit of God because we believe, but that we may believe.

FULGENTIUS OF RUSPE

He leadeth me, O blessed thought,
O words with heavenly comfort fraught,
Whate'er I do, where'er I be,
Still 'tis God's hand that leadeth me.

JOSEPH HENRY GILMORE

Our Walk

counts far more than

Our Talk,

always!

GEORGE MÜLLER

Faith IS THE SUBTLE CHAIN which BINDS US TO THE Infinite.

ELIZABETH OAKS SMITH

How goodness heightens beauty!

HANNAH MORE

It is neither wealth nor splendor, but tranquility and
occupation which give happiness.

THOMAS JEFFERSON

It is not what he has, nor even what he does, which directly
expresses the worth of a man, but what he is.

HENRI-FRÉDÉRIC AMIEL

One word frees us of all the weight and pain of life:
That word is love.

SOPHOCLES

Mistake not. Those pleasures are not pleasures that trouble the quiet and tranquillity of thy life.

JEREMY TAYLOR

Gracefulness has been defined to be the outward expression of the inward harmony of the soul.

WILLIAM HAZLITT

In all ranks of life the human heart yearns for the beautiful; and the beautiful things that God makes are His gift to all alike.

HARRIET BEECHER STOWE

Trust and have faith!

REASON SAW NOT,
Till Faith
SPRUNG THE LIGHT.

John Dryden

I SEE HEAVEN'S
GLORIES SHINE
& faith shines
EQUAL.

EMILY BRONTË

Let us then be up and doing,
With a heart for any fate;
Still achieving, still pursuing,
Learn to labor and to wait.

HENRY WADSWORTH LONGFELLOW

Happy am I; from care I'm free!
Why aren't they all contented like me?

OPERA OF LA BAYADÈRE

Just as there comes a warm sunbeam
into every cottage window, so comes
a love beam of God's care and
pity for every separate need.

NATHANIEL HAWTHORNE

Depend upon it. God's work done in God's way will never lack God's supplies.

J. HUDSON TAYLOR

Let him have all your worries and cares, for he is always thinking about you and watching everything that concerns you.

1 PETER 5:7

My profession is always to be alert, to find God in nature, to know God's lurking places, to attend to all the oratorios and the operas in nature.

HENRY DAVID THOREAU

Attempt GREAT THINGS FOR GOD, Expect GREAT THINGS FROM GOD.

WRITE IT ON YOUR *Heart* THAT **EVERY DAY** IS THE *Best Day* IN THE YEAR.

RALPH WALDO EMERSON

Put together all the tenderest love you know of,
the deepest you have ever felt, and the strongest
that has ever been poured out upon you, and heap
upon it all the love of all the loving human hearts in
the world, and then multiply it by infinity, and
you will begin, perhaps, to have some faint glimpse
of what the love of God is.

HANNAH WHITALL SMITH

God passes through the thicket of the world,
and wherever his glance falls he turns all
things to beauty.

JOHN OF THE CROSS

Boldly and wisely in that
light thou hast—
There is a hand above
will help thee on.

PHILIP JAMES BAILEY

There is only one way to happiness and that is to cease worrying about things which are beyond the power of our will.

EPICTETUS

Adversity is the diamond dust heaven polishes its jewels with.

ROBERT LEIGHTON

O God, my heart is quiet and confident… Your kindness and love are as vast as the heavens. Your faithfulness is higher than the skies.

PSALM 57:7,10

He is Rich or Poor

ACCORDING TO WHAT HE IS, NOT ACCORDING TO WHAT HE HAS.

HENRY WARD BEECHER

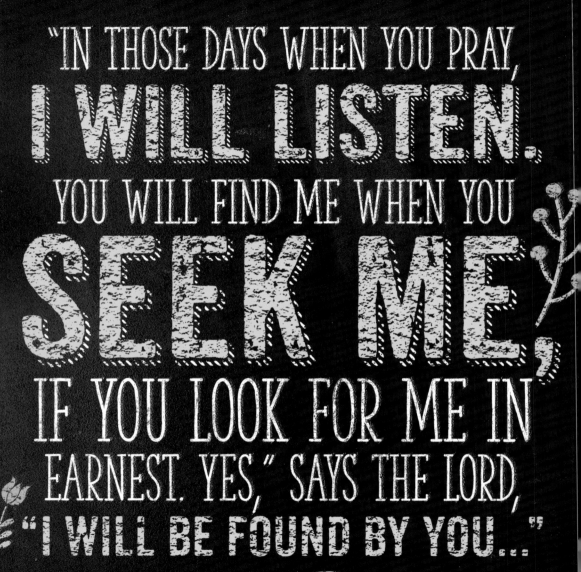

"IN THOSE DAYS WHEN YOU PRAY, I WILL LISTEN. YOU WILL FIND ME WHEN YOU SEEK ME, IF YOU LOOK FOR ME IN EARNEST. YES," SAYS THE LORD, "I WILL BE FOUND BY YOU..."

JEREMIAH 29:12-14